T0041444

A NATURE POEM FOR
EVERY WINTER EVENING

A NATURE POEM FOR EVERY WINTER EVENING

EDITED BY *Jane McMorland Hunter*

First published in the United Kingdom in 2022 by
B.T. Batsford Ltd
43 Great Ormond Street
London WC1N 3HZ
An imprint of B.T. Batsford Holdings Ltd

Copyright © B.T. Batsford Ltd 2022

All rights reserved. No part of this publication may be
copied, displayed, extracted, reproduced, utilised, stored in a
retrieval system or transmitted in any form or by any means,
electronic, mechanical or otherwise including but not limited
to photocopying, recording, or scanning without the prior
written permission of the publishers.

ISBN 9781849947985

A CIP catalogue record for this book is available from the
British Library.

10 9 8 7 6 5 4 3 2
35 34 33 32 31 30 29 28 27 26 25 24 23

Reproduction by Rival Colour Ltd, UK
Printed by Elma Basim, Turkey

This book can be ordered direct from the publisher at
www.batsfordbooks.com

CONTENTS

To Matilda, who came home. And to Mat
and Sarah, who helped. With all my love.

ABOUT THE EDITOR

Jane McMorland Hunter has compiled
11 anthologies of poetry for Batsford and the
National Trust. She also writes gardening and
cookery books and works as a gardener and at
Hatchards bookshop in Piccadilly. She lives in
London with a small, grey tabby cat.

Introduction

Evening marks the point where day slips into night and our view of the natural world changes. Midnight may mark the change from one day to the next but evening marks the end or close of the day. The sun sinks, dusk or twilight sets in and the natural world moves towards one which is subtly lit by stars and moonlight. Things appear less clearly and what was certain by daylight becomes less sure; as Amy Lowell says, 'the moonlight deceives'. This is part of evening's charm and, even when the moon and stars are hidden from sight, the darkened world is both mysterious and beguiling. It is a good time to reflect on the day that has passed and look forward to the one to come, and the perfect time to allow one's imagination to take flight in the company of a poet.

I strongly believe there are two winters: one the reality, the other that which resides in our minds, our memories and our imaginations. Here snow does not bring the country to a grinding halt but lies – deep and crisp and even

– surely one of the most beautiful phrases in the English language. Winter may be a time of short days and icy winds but it is also the season of glittering icicles, atmospheric mists and impressive storms. Nature is at both her most majestic and her most subtle.

The start of winter still holds onto a touch of autumn but everything changes with the first frost. In poetry this, along with snow and storms, can arrive at the correct moment and provide beauty rather than inconvenience. Sara Teasdale describes frost as 'feathery filigree' and James Russell Lowell sees snow as rich ermine or fine pearls adorning the trees. Images of magical wedding cakes and trees wearing soft white gloves leap off the page to bring joy to the dampest evening. Regardless of the weather outside, these images can be enjoyed and make the reality of winter less harsh. Even storms such as that described by George Crabbe where 'one cloud, / Black and unbroken, all the skies o'ershroud' can be relished from a comfortable armchair.

For many people December is dominated by Christmas; first the preparations and then the celebrations themselves. Whatever one's view of this, each day it is heartening to step back and realise that, for the natural world no such distractions exist; winds blow, stars twinkle and clouds billow regardless of the calendar date.

January is the turning point of the year, even if not from the practical point of winter. It is now that people, poets and nature begin to look forward to the promise of warmth and its attendant joys. January 22nd, St Vincent's Day, is a crucial date – with the certainty beloved of folklore and poetry, it is said that if the sun appears on this day then the whole year will be assured good weather.

By February nature has moved to a state so well described by Mary Webb as 'Not yet'. Early February can feel like the deepest point of winter, just as midnight is the darkest hour of night but, as Louisa Bevington reminds us, 'There is action in the stillness, / There is progress in the dark'. Even in the depths of winter there is new life with snowdrops and the songs of hardy birds brightening the times. And there is much to love in winter; Emily Brontë likes it as much as summer and for William Cullen Bryant it boasts splendours greater than any the other seasons can aspire to.

Finally the West Wind brings a gentler air, the thrush sings of a world born anew and then, suddenly, there is a perfect day. The date in this anthology is the 21st February but you should seize it whenever it comes. Go out, make the most of it but, come the evening, return to your chair by the fire. For it is not summer yet. By the end of the month the poets are looking for signs of spring. The collection ends with buds, frogs, violets and a brightness in the air but, for me, the most evocative sign of the end of winter and probably my favourite piece in the entire collection is the short poem 'Thaw' by Edward Thomas:

Over the land freckled with snow half-thawed
The speculating rooks at their nests cawed
And saw from the elm-tops, delicate as flower
   of grass,
What we could not see, Winter pass.

DECEMBER

A Silence Deep and White

1ST DECEMBER

First Day of Winter

Like the bloom on a grape is the evening air
And a first faint frost the wind has bound.
Yet the fear of his breath avails to scare
The withered leaves on the cold ground.

For they huddle and whisper in phantom throngs,
I hear them beneath the branches bare:
We danced with the Wind, we sang his songs;
Now he pursues us, we know not where.

Laurence Binyon (1869–1943)

2ᴺᴰ DECEMBER

The Induction

The wrathful winter, 'proaching on apace,
　With blustering blasts had all ybared the treen,
And old Saturnus, with his frosty face,
　With chilling cold had pierced the tender green;
　The mantles rent, wherein enwrapped been
　　The gladsome groves that now lay overthrown,
　　The tapets torn, and every bloom down blown.

The soil, that erst so seemly was to seen,
　Was all despoiled of her beauty's hue;
And soote fresh flowers, wherewith the
　　　　　　　　　　　　summer's queen
　Had clad the earth, now Boreas' blasts
　　　　　　　　　　down blew;
　And small fowls flocking, in their song did rue
　The winter's wrath, wherewith each
　　　　　　　　　　thing defaced
　In woeful wise bewailed the summer past.

Hawthorn had lost his motley livery,
  The naked twigs were shivering all for cold,
And dropping down the tears abundantly;
  Each thing, methought, with weeping eye me told
  The cruel season, bidding me withhold
    Myself within; for I was gotten out
    Into the fields, whereas I walked about.

Thomas Sackville (1536–1608)

3RD DECEMBER

The Moon was but a Chin of Gold

The Moon was but a Chin of Gold
A Night or two ago –
And now she turns Her perfect Face
Upon the World below –

Her Forehead is of Amplest Blonde -
Her Cheek – a Beryl hewn –
Her Eye unto the Summer Dew
The likest I have known -–

Her Lips of Amber never part –
But what must be the smile
Upon Her Friend she could confer
Were such Her Silver Will –

And what a privilege to be
But the remotest Star –
For Certainty She take Her Way
Beside Your Palace Door –

Her Bonnet is the Firmament –
The Universe – Her Shoe –
The Stars – the Trinkets at Her Belt –
Her Dimities –of Blue –

Emily Dickinson (1830–1886)

4TH DECEMBER

The Retired Cat

A poet's cat, sedate and grave
As poet well could wish to have,
Was much addicted to inquire
For nooks, to which she might retire,
And where, secure as mouse in chink,
She might repose, or sit and think.
I know not where she caught the trick –
Nature perhaps herself had cast her
In such a mould PHILOSOPHIQUE,
Or else she learn'd it of her master.
Sometimes ascending, debonair,
An apple-tree or lofty pear,
Lodg'd with convenience in the fork,
She watched the gard'ner at his work;
Sometimes her ease and solace sought
In an old empty wat'ring-pot,
There, wanting nothing save a fan,
To seem some nymph in her sedan,
Apparell'd in exactest sort,
And ready to be borne to court.

   But love of change, it seems, has place
Not only in our wiser race;
Cats also feel as well as we

That passion's force, and so did she.
Her climbing, she began to find,
Expos'd her too much to the wind,
And the old utensil of tin
Was cold and comfortless within:
She therefore wish'd instead of those
Some place of more serene repose,
Where neither cold might come, nor air
Too rudely wanton with her hair,
And sought it in the likeliest mode
Within her master's snug abode.
All if poss, cut here if necessary

   A draw'r, – it chanc'd, at bottom lin'd
With linen of the softest kind,
With such as merchants introduce
From India, for the ladies' use, –
A draw'r impending o'er the rest,
Half-open in the topmost chest,
Of depth enough, and none to spare,
Invited her to slumber there;
Puss with delight beyond expression
Survey'd the scene, and took possession.
Recumbent at her ease ere long,
And lull'd by her own hum-drum song,
She left the cares of life behind,

And slept as she would sleep her last,
When in came, housewifely inclin'd,
The chambermaid, and shut it fast,
By no malignity impell'd,
But all unconscious whom it held.

   Awaken'd by the shock (cried puss)
Was ever cat attended thus!
The open draw'r was left, I see,
Merely to prove a nest for me.
For soon as I was well compos'd,
Then came the maid, and it was closed:
How smooth these 'kerchiefs, and how sweet,
O what a delicate retreat!
I will resign myself to rest
Till Sol, declining in the west,
Shall call to supper; when, no doubt,
Susan will come and let me out.

   The evening came, the sun descended,
And puss remain'd still unattended.
The night roll'd tardily away,
(With her indeed 'twas never day)
The sprightly morn her course renew'd,
The evening gray again ensued,
And puss came into mind no more
Than if entomb'd the day before.

With hunger pinch'd, and pinch'd for room,
She now presag'd approaching doom,
Nor slept a single wink, or purr'd,
Conscious of jeopardy incurr'd.

   That night, by chance, the poet watching
Heard an inexplicable scratching,
His noble heart went pit-a-pat
And to himself he said – what's that?
He drew the curtain at his side,
And forth he peep'd, but nothing spied.
Yet, by his ear directed, guess'd
Something imprison'd in the chest,
And doubtful what, with prudent care
Resolv'd it should continue there.
At length a voice which well he knew,
A long and melancholy mew,
Saluting his poetic ears,
Consol'd him, and dispell'd his fears;
He left his bed, he trod the floor,
He 'gan in haste the draw'rs explore,
The lowest first, and without stop,
The rest in order to the top;
For 'tis a truth well known to most,
That whatsoever thing is lost,
We seek it, ere it come to light,

In ev'ry cranny but the right.
Forth skipp'd the cat; not now replete
As erst with airy self-conceit,
Nor in her own fond apprehension,
A theme for all the world's attention,
But modest, sober, cur'd of all
Her notions hyperbolical,
And wishing for a place of rest
Any thing rather than a chest.
Then stept the poet into bed,
With this reflexion in his head:

MORAL

Beware of too sublime a sense
Of your own worth and consequence!
The man who dreams himself so great,
And his importance of such weight,
That all around, in all that's done
Must move and act for him alone,
Will learn, in school of tribulation
The folly of his expectation.

William Cowper (1731–1800)

5TH DECEMBER

Nightpiece

Gaunt in gloom,
The pale stars their torches,
Enshrouded, wave.
Ghostfires from heaven's far verges faint illume,
Arches on soaring arches,
Night's sindark nave.

Seraphim,
The lost hosts awaken
To service till
In moonless gloom each lapses muted, dim,
Raised when she has and shaken
Her thurible.

And long and loud,
To night's nave upsoaring,
A starknell tolls
As the bleak incense surges, cloud on cloud,
Voidward from the adoring
Waste of souls.

James Joyce (1882–1941)

6ᵀᴴ DECEMBER

Winter-Time

Late lies the wintry sun a-bed,
A frosty, fiery sleepy-head;
Blinks but an hour or two; and then,
A blood-red orange, sets again.

Before the stars have left the skies,
At morning in the dark I rise;
And shivering in my nakedness,
By the cold candle, bathe and dress.

Close by the jolly fire I sit
To warm my frozen bones a bit;
Or with a reindeer-sled, explore
The colder countries round the door.

When to go out, my nurse doth wrap
Me in my comforter and cap;
The cold wind burns my face, and blows
Its frosty pepper up my nose.

Black are my steps on silver sod;
Thick blows my frosty breath abroad;
And tree and house, and hill and lake,
Are frosted like a wedding-cake.

Robert Louis Stevenson (1850–1894)

7TH DECEMBER

A Beech

They will not go. These leaves insist on staying.
Coinage like theirs looked frail six weeks ago.
What hintings at, excitement of delaying,
Almost as if some richer fruits could grow

If leaves hung on against each swipe of storm,
If branches bent but still did not give way.
Today is brushed with sun. The leaves are warm.
I picked one from the pavement and it lay

With borrowed shining on my Winter hand.
Persistence of this nature sends the pulse
Beating more rapidly. When will it end,

That pride of leaves? When will the branches be
Utterly bare, and seem like something else,
Now half-forgotten, no part of a tree?

Elizabeth Jennings (1926–2001)

8TH DECEMBER

General Description

FROM *THE BOROUGH*, LINES 194–213

View now the winter-storm! above, one cloud,
Black and unbroken, all the skies o'ershroud:
Th' unwieldy porpoise through the day before
Had roll'd in view of boding men on shore;
And sometimes hid and sometimes show'd
  his form,
Dark as the cloud, and furious as the storm.
All where the eye delights, yet dreads to roam,
The breaking billows cast the flying foam
Upon the billows rising – all the deep
Is restless change; the waves so swell'd and steep,
Breaking and sinking, and the sunken swells,
Nor one, one moment, in its station dwells:
But nearer land you may the billows trace,
As if contending in their watery chase;
May watch the mightiest till the shoal they reach,
Then break and hurry to their utmost stretch;
Curl'd as they come, they strike with
  furious force,
And then re-flowing, take their grating course,
Raking the rounded flints, which ages past
Roll'd by their rage, and shall to ages last.

George Crabbe (1754–1832)

9TH DECEMBER

Frost at Midnight

LINES 1–16

The Frost performs its secret ministry,
Unhelped by any wind. The owlet's cry
Came loud – and hark, again! loud as before.
The inmates of my cottage, all at rest,
Have left me to that solitude, which suits
Abtruser musings: save that at my side
My cradled infant slumbers peacefully.
'Tis calm indeed! so calm, that it disturbs
And vexes meditation with its strange
And extreme stillness. Sea, hill, and wood,
This populous village! Sea, and hill, and wood,
With all the numberless goings-on of life,
Inaudible as dreams! the thin blue flame
Lies on my low-burnt fire, and quivers not;
Only that film, which fluttered on the grate,
Still flutters there, the sole unquiet thing.

Samuel Taylor Coleridge (1772–1834)

10TH DECEMBER

There Was a Boy

There was a boy – ye knew him well, ye cliffs
And islands of Winander – many a time
At evening, when the stars had just begun
To move along the edges of the hills,
Rising or setting, would he stand alone
Beneath the trees or by the glimmering lake,
And there, with fingers interwoven, both hands
Pressed closely palm to palm and to his mouth
Uplifted, he, as though an instrument,
Blew mimic hootings to the silent owls,
That they might answer him. And they
   would shout
Across the watery vale, and shout again,
Responsive to his call, with quavering peals,
And long halloos, and screams, and echoes loud,
Redoubled and redoubled – a wild scene
Of mirth and jocund din. And when it chanced
That pauses of deep silence mocked his skill,
Then sometimes in that silence, while he hung
Listening, a gentle shock of mild surprise
Has carried far into his heart the voice
Of mountain torrents; or the visible scene

Would enter unawares into his mind
With all its solemn imagery – its rocks,
Its woods, and that uncertain heaven – received
Into the bosom of the steady lake.

William Wordsworth (1770–1850)

11ᵀᴴ DECEMBER

Earth to Earth

VERSES 1 AND 2

Where the region grows without a lord,
  Between the thickets emerald-stoled,
In the woodland bottom the virgin sward,
    The cream of the earth, through depths of mold
      O'erflowing wells from secret cells,
While the moon and the sun keep watch and ward,
And the ancient world is never old.

Here, alone, by the grass-green hearth
  Tarry a little: the mood will come!
Feel your body a part of earth;
  Rest and quicken your thought at home;
    Take your ease with the brooding trees;
Join in their deep-down silent mirth
  The crumbling rock and the fertile loam.

John Davidson (1857–1909)

12TH DECEMBER

Trees

The Oak is called the king of trees,
The Aspen quivers in the breeze,
The Poplar grows up straight and tall,
The Peach-tree spreads along the wall,
The Sycamore gives pleasant shade,
The Willow droops in watery glade,
The Fir-tree useful timber gives,
The Beech amid the Forest lives.

Sara Coleridge (1802–1852)

13TH DECEMBER

How still, how happy!

How still, how happy! Those are words
That once would scarce agree together;
I loved the plashing of the surge –
The changing heaven the breezy weather,

More than smooth seas and cloudless skies
And solemn, soothing, softened airs
That in the forest woke no sighs
And from the green spray shook no tears.

How still, how happy! Now I feel
Where silence dwells is sweeter far
Than laughing mirth's most joyous swell
However pure its raptures are.

Come, sit down on this sunny stone:
'Tis wintry light o'er flowerless moors –
But sit – for we are all alone
And clear expand heaven's breathless shores.

I could think in the withered grass
Spring's budding wreaths we might discern;
The violet's eye might shyly flash
And young leaves shoot among the fern.

It is but thought – full many a night
The snow shall clothe those hills afar
And storms shall add a drearier blight
And winds shall wage a wilder war,

Before the lark may herald in
Fresh foliage twined with blossoms fair
And summer days again begin
Their glory-haloed crown to wear.

Yet my heart loves December's smile
As much as July's golden beam;
Then let us sit and watch the while
The blue ice curdling on the stream.

Emily Brontë (1818–1848)

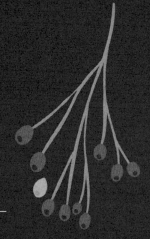

14ᵀᴴ DECEMBER

The First Snow-Fall

VERSES 1–4

The snow had begun in the gloaming,
   And busily all the night
Had been heaping field and highway
   With a silence deep and white.

Every pine and fir and hemlock
   Wore ermine too dear for an earl,
And the poorest twig on the elm-tree
   Was ridged inch deep with pearl.

From sheds new-roofed with Carrara
   Came Chanticleer's muffled crow,
The stiff rails softened to swan's-down,
   And still fluttered down the snow.

I stood and watched by the window
   The noiseless work of the sky,
And the sudden flurries of snowbirds,
   Like brown leaves whirling by.

James Russell Lowell (1819–1891)

15TH DECEMBER

A December Day

Dawn turned on her purple pillow
  And late, late came the winter day,
Snow was curved to the boughs of the willow.
  The sunless world was white and grey.

At noon we heard a blue-jay scolding,
  At five the last thin light was lost
From snow-banked windows faintly holding
  The feathery filigree of frost.

Sara Teasdale (1884–1933)

16TH DECEMBER

Winter's Beauty

Is it not fine to walk in spring,
When leaves are born, and hear birds sing?
And when they lose their singing powers,
In summer, watch the bees at flowers?
Is it not fine, when summer's past,
To have the leaves, no longer fast,
Biting my heel where'er I go,
Or dancing lightly on my toe?
Now winter's here and rivers freeze;
As I walk out I see the trees,
Wherein the pretty squirrels sleep,
All standing in the snow so deep:
And every twig, however small,
Is blossomed white and beautiful.
Then welcome, winter, with thy power
To make this tree a big white flower;
To make this tree a lovely sight,
With fifty brown arms draped in white,
While thousands of small fingers show
In soft white gloves of purest snow.

W. H. Davies (1871–1940)

17TH DECEMBER

The Winter Evening

THE TASK, BOOK IV, LINES 311–332

I saw the woods and fields, at close of day,
A variegated show; the meadows green,
Though faded; and the lands, where lately wav'd
The golden harvest, of a mellow brown,
Upturn'd so lately by the forceful share.
I saw far off the weedy fallows smile
With verdure not unprofitable, graz'd
By flocks, fast-feeding, and selecting each
His fav'rite herb; while all the leafless groves,
That skirt th' horizon, wore a sable hue,
Scarce notic'd in the kindred dusk of eve.
To-morrow brings a change, a total change!
Which even now, though silently perform'd,
And slowly, and by most unfelt, the face
Of universal nature undergoes.
Fast falls a fleecy show'r: the downy flakes,
Descending, and with never-ceasing lapse,
Softly alighting upon all below,
Assimilate all objects. Earth receives

Gladly the thick'ning mantle; and the green
And tender blade that fear'd the chilling blast,
Escapes unhurt beneath so warm a veil.

William Cowper (1731–1800)

18TH DECEMBER

Stars Sliding

The stars are sliding wanton through trees,
   The sky is sliding steady over all.
Great Bear to Gemini will lose his place
   And Cygnus over world's brink slip and fall.

Follow-my-Leader's not so bad a game.
   But were it Leap Frog: O! to see the shoots
And tracks of glory; Scorpions and Swans tame
   And Argo swarmed with Bulls and other brutes.

Ivor Gurney (1890–1937)

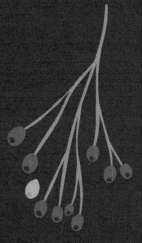

19TH DECEMBER

To the Evening Star

Gem of the crimson-colour'd Even,
Companion of retiring day,
Why at the closing gates of heaven,
Beloved Star, dost thou delay?

So fair thy pensile beauty burns
When soft the tear of twilight flows;
So due thy plighted love returns
To chambers brighter than the rose;

To Peace, to Pleasure, and to Love
So kind a star thou seem'st to be,
Sure some enamour'd orb above
Descends and burns to meet with thee!

Thine is the breathing, blushing hour
When all unheavenly passions fly,
Chased by the soul-subduing power
Of Love's delicious witchery.

Thomas Campbell (1777–1844)

20TH DECEMBER

Stopping by Woods
on a Snowy Evening

Whose woods these are I think I know.
His house is in the village though;
He will not see me stopping here
To watch his woods fill up with snow.

My little horse must think it queer
To stop without a farmhouse near
Between the woods and frozen lake
The darkest evening of the year.

He gives his harness bells a shake
To ask if there is some mistake.
The only other sound's the sweep
Of easy wind and downy flake.

The woods are lovely, dark and deep,
But I have promises to keep,
And miles to go before I sleep.
And miles to go before I sleep.

Robert Frost (1874–1963)

21ST DECEMBER

Moon Haze

Because the moonlight deceives
Therefore I love it.

Amy Lowell (1874–1925)

22ND DECEMBER

Childe Harold's Pilgrimage

CANTO THE FOURTH

CLXXVIII

There is a pleasure in the pathless woods,
There is a rapture on the lonely shore,
There is society, where none intrudes,
By the deep Sea, and music in its roar:
I love not Man the less, but Nature more,
From these our interviews, in which I steal
From all I may be, or have been before,
To mingle with the Universe, and feel
What I can ne'er express, yet cannot all conceal.

Lord George Gordon Byron (1788–1824)

23RD DECEMBER

Through Springtime Walks

Through springtime walks, with flowers perfumed,
   I chased a wild capricious fair,
Where hyacinths and jonquils bloomed,
   Chanting gay sonnets through the air;
     Hid amid a briary dell
       Or 'neath a hawthorn-tree,
      Her sweet enchantments led me on
        And still deluded me.

While summer's 'splendent glory smiles
   My ardent love in vain essayed,
I strove to win her heart by wiles,
   But still a thousand pranks she played;
Still o'er each sunburnt furzy hill,
   Wild, playful, gay, and free,
She laughed and scorned; I chased her still,
   And still she bantered me.

When autumn waves her golden ears
  And wafts o'er fruits her pregnant breath,
The sprightly lark its pinions rears;
  I chased her o'er the daisied heath,
And all around was glee –
Still, wanton as the timid hart,
  She swiftly flew from me.

Now winter lights its cheerful fire,
  While jests with frolic mirth resound
And draws the wandering beauty nigher,
  'Tis now too cold to rove around;
The Christmas-game, the playful dance,
  Incline her heart to glee –
Mutual we glow, and kindling love
  Draws every wish to me.

Ann Batten Cristall (1769–1848)

24TH DECEMBER

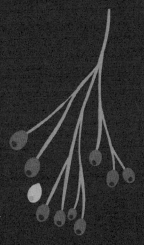

Arracombe Wood

Some said, because he wud'n spaik
　　Any words to women but Yes and No,
Nor put out his hand for Parson to shake
　　He mun be bird-witted. But I do go
　　By the lie of the barley that he did sow,
And I wish for no better thing than to hold a rake
　　Like Dave, in his time, or to see him mow.

Put up in the churchyard a month ago,
'A bitter old soul,' they said, but it wadn't so.
His heart were in Arracombe Wood where he'd
　　　　　　　　used to go
To sit and talk wi' his shadder till sun went low,
Thought what it was all about us'll never know.
　　And thee baint no mem'ry in the place
　　Of th' old man's footmark, nor his face;
　　Arracombe Wood do think more of a crow –
'Will be violets there in the Spring: in Summer
　　　　　　　　time the spider's lace;
　　And come the Fall, the whizzle and race
Of the dry, dead leaves when the wind gies chase;
　　And on the Eve of Christmas, fallin' snow.

Charlotte Mew (1869–1928)

25TH DECEMBER

Christmas Night

Softly, softly, through the darkness
   Snow is falling.
Sharply, sharply, in the meadows
   Lambs are calling.
Coldly, coldly, all around me
   Winds are blowing.
Brightly, brightly, up above me
   Stars are glowing.

Anon

26TH DECEMBER

Winter Trees on the Horizon

O delicate! Even in wooded lands
   They show the margin of my world,
My own horizon; little bands
   Of twigs unveil that edge impearled,

And what is more mine own than this –
   My limit, level with mine eyes?
For me precisely do they kiss –
   The rounded earth, the rounding skies.

It has my stature, that keen line
   (Let mathematics vouch for it).
The lark's horizon is not mine,
   No, nor his nestlings' where they sit;

No, nor the child's. And, when I gain
   The hills, I lift it as I rise
Erect; anon, back to the plain
   I soothe it with mine equal eyes.

Alice Meynell (1847–1922)

27TH DECEMBER

Rose-berries

The green pine-needles shiver glassily,
Each cased in ice. Harsh winter, grey and dun,
Shuts out the sun.
But with live, scarlet fire,
Enfolding seed of sweet Junes yet to be,
Rose-berries melt the snow, and burn above
The thorny briar,
Like beauty with its deathless seed of love.

Mary Webb (1881–1927)

28TH DECEMBER

Winter Branches

Against the smoke-browned wall
The browner winter branches
Stand out hardly at all;
They do not tremble in the misty evening.

But under the open sky
Where the stars in clear and tranquil
Sufficiency go by,
They leap up quivering into the vastness

Like flame, like the thought of man
Leaping from earth's nurture,
Through span on alien span,
To tremble around the stars its kindred.

Nan Shepherd (1893–1981)

29TH DECEMBER

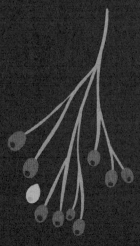

The Cat

Within that porch, across the way,
  I see two naked eyes this night;
Two eyes that neither shut nor blink,
  Searching my face with a green light.

But cats to me are strange, so strange –
  I cannot sleep if one is near;
And though I'm sure I see those eyes,
  I'm not so sure a body's there!

W. H. Davies (1871–1940)

30TH DECEMBER

Snowbound: A Winter Idyl, 1865

LINES 1–18

The sun that brief December day
Rose cheerless over hills of gray,
And, darkly circled, gave at noon
A sadder light than waning moon.
Slow tracing down the thickening sky
Its mute and ominous prophecy,
A portent seeming less than threat,
It sank from sight before it set.
A chill no coat, however stout,
Of homespun stuff could quite shut out,
A hard, dull bitterness of cold,
    That checked, mid-vein, the circling race
    Of life-blood in the sharpened face,
The coming of the snow-storm told.
The wind blew east; we heard the roar
Of Ocean on his wintry shore,
And felt the strong pulse throbbing there
Beat with low rhythm our inland air.

John Greenleaf Whittier (1807–1892)

31ST DECEMBER

The Darkling Thrush

I leant upon a coppice gate
   When Frost was spectre-gray,
And Winter's dregs made desolate
   The weakening eye of day.
The tangled bine-stems scored the sky
   Like strings of broken lyres,
And all mankind that haunted nigh
   Had sought their household fires.

The land's sharp features seemed to be
   The Century's corpse outleant,
His crypt the cloudy canopy,
   The wind his death-lament.
The ancient pulse of germ and birth
   Was shrunken hard and dry,
And every spirit upon earth
   Seemed fervourless as I.

At once a voice arose among
   The bleak twigs overhead
In a full-hearted evensong
   Of joy illimited;
An aged thrush, frail, gaunt, and small,
   In blast-beruffled plume,
Had chosen thus to fling his soul
   Upon the growing gloom.

So little cause for carolings
   Of such ecstatic sound
Was written on terrestrial things
   Afar or nigh around,
That I could think there trembled through
   His happy good-night air
Some blessed Hope, whereof he knew
   And I was unaware.

Thomas Hardy (1840–1928)

JANUARY

The Stars were Sparkling Clear

1ˢᵀ JANUARY

Tapestry Trees

Oak.
I am the Roof-tree and the Keel;
I bridge the seas for woe and weal.

Fir.
High o'er the lordly oak I stand,
And drive him on from land to land.

Ash.
I heft my brother's iron bane;
I shaft the spear, and build the wain.

Yew.
Dark down the windy dale I grow,
The father of the fateful Bow.

Poplar.
The war-shaft and the milking-bowl
I make, and keep the hay-wain whole.

Olive.
The King I bless; the lamps I trim;
In my warm wave do fishes swim.

Apple-tree.
I bowed my head to Adam's will;
The cups of toiling men I fill.

Vine.
I draw the blood from out the earth;
I store the sun for winter mirth.

Orange-tree.
Amidst the greenness of my night,
My odorous lamps hang round and bright.

Fig-tree.
I who am little among trees
In honey-making mate the bees.

Mulberry-tree.
Love's lack hath dyed my berries red:
For Love' attire my leaves are shed.

Pear-tree.

High o'er the mead-flowers' hidden feet
I bear aloft my burden sweet.

Bay.

Look on my leafy boughs, the Crown
Of living song and dead renown!

William Morris (1834–1896)

2ND JANUARY

The Months

January brings the snow,
Makes our feet and fingers glow.

February brings the rain,
Thaws the frozen lake again.

March brings breezes loud and shrill,
Stirs the dancing daffodil.

April brings the primrose sweet,
Scatters daises at our feet.

May brings flocks of pretty lambs,
Skipping by their fleecy dams.

June brings tulips, lilies, roses,
Fills the children's hand with posies.

Hot July brings cooling showers,
Apricots and gillyflowers.

August brings the sheaves of corn,
Then the harvest home is borne.

Warm September brings the fruit,
Sportsmen then begin to shoot.

Fresh October brings the pheasant,
Then to gather nuts is pleasant.

Dull November brings the blast,
Then the leaves are whirling fast.

Chill December brings the sleet,
Blazing fire, and Christmas treat.

Sara Coleridge (1802–1852)

3RD JANUARY

Sonnet: The Human Seasons

Four seasons fill the measure of the year;
　There are four seasons in the mind of man:
He has his lusty Spring, when fancy clear
　Takes in all beauty with an easy span:
He has his Summer, when luxuriously
　Spring's honied cud of youthful thought he loves
To ruminate, and by such dreaming high
　Is nearest unto heaven: quiet coves
His soul has in its Autumn, when his wings
　He furleth close; contented so to look
On mists in idleness – to let fair things
　　Pass by unheeded as a threshold brook.
He has his Winter too of pale misfeature,
Or else he would forego his mortal nature.

John Keats (1795–1821)

4TH JANUARY

A Dream of Summer

VERSES 1–3

Bland as the morning breath of June
  The southwest breezes play;
And, through its haze, the winter noon
  Seems warm as summer's day.
The snow-plumed Angel of the North
  Has dropped his icy spear;
Again the mossy earth looks forth,
  Again the streams gush clear.

The fox his hillside cell forsakes,
  The muskrat leaves his nook,
The bluebird in the meadow brakes
  Is singing with the brook.
'Bear up, O Mother Nature!' cry
  Bird, breeze, and streamlet free;
'Our winter voices prophesy
  Of summer days to thee!'

So, in those winters of the soul,
  By bitter blasts and drear
O'erswept from Memory's frozen pole,
  Will sunny days appear.
Reviving Hope and Faith, they show
  The soul its living powers,
And how beneath the winter's snow
  Lie germs of summer flowers!

John Greenleaf Whittier (1807–1892)

5ᵀᴴ JANUARY

Sonnet 60

Like as the waves make towards the pebbled shore,
So do our minutes hasten to their end;
Each changing place with that which goes before,
In sequent toil all forwards do contend.
Nativity, once in the main of light,
Crawls to maturity, wherewith being crowned,
Crooked eclipses 'gainst his glory fight,
And Time that gave doth now his gift confound.
Time doth transfix the flourish set on youth
And delves the parallels in beauty's brow,
Feeds on the rarities of nature's truth,
And nothing stands but for his scythe to mow:
   And yet to times in hope my verse shall stand,
   Praising thy worth, despite his cruel hand.

William Shakespeare (1564–1616)

6ᵀᴴ JANUARY

Not So Far as the Forest

I

That chill is in the air
Which the wise know well, and even have
    learned to bear.
This joy, I know,
Will soon be under snow.

The sun sets in a cloud
And is not seen.
Beauty, that spoke aloud,
Addresses now only the remembering ear.
The heart begins here
To feed on what has been.

Night falls fast.
Today is in the past.

Blown from the dark hill hither to my door
Three flakes, then four
Arrive, then many more.

Edna St Vincent Millay (1892–1950)

7TH JANUARY

The Night of the Dance

The cold moon hangs to the sky by its horn
   And centres its gaze on me;
The stars, like eyes in reverie,
Their westering as for a while forborne,
   Quiz downward curiously.

Old Robert draws the backbrand in,
   The green logs steam and spit;
The half-awakened sparrows flit
From the riddled thatch; and owls begin
   To whoo from the gable-slit.

Yes; far and nigh things seem to know
   Sweet scenes are impending here;
That all is prepared; that the hour is near
For welcomes, fellowships, and flow
   Of sally, song, and cheer;

That spigots are pulled and viols strung;
   That soon will arise the sound
Of measures trod to tunes renowned;
That She will return in Love's low tongue
   My vows as we wheel around.

Thomas Hardy (1840–1928)

8TH JANUARY

The Lake

On a calm day
The lake
Imagines it is a mirror
And smiles back
At people who pass by
Smiling.

On a breezy day
The lake
Hunches its shoulders
And sends ripples
Scudding across the surface.

On a winter's day
The lake
Hides itself
Under a frozen blanket
And refuses to budge
Until it is warm enough
To come out again.

John Foster (1941–)

9TH JANUARY

Impressions I

LES SILHOUETTES

The sea is flecked with bars of grey
The dull dead wind is out of tune,
And like a withered leaf the moon
Is blown across the stormy bay.

Etched clear upon the pallid sand
The black boat lies: a sailor boy
Clambers aboard in careless joy
With laughing face and gleaming hand.

And overheard the curlews cry,
Where through the dusky upland grass
The young brown-throated reapers pass,
Like silhouettes against the sky.

Oscar Wilde (1854–1900)

10TH JANUARY

10TH JANUARY

Trees

I think that I shall never see
A poem as lovely as a tree.

A tree whose hungry mouth is prest
Against the earth's sweet flowing breast;

A tree that looks at God all day,
And lifts her leafy arms to pray;

A tree that may in Summer wear
A nest of robins in her hair;

Upon whose bosom snow has lain
Who intimately lives with rain.

Poems are made by fools like me,
But only God can make a tree.

Joyce Kilmer (1886–1918)

11TH JANUARY

Sonnet IV: To the Moon

Queen of the silver bow! - by thy pale beam,
  Alone and pensive, I delight to stray,
And watch thy shadow trembling in the stream,
  Or mark the floating clouds that cross thy way.
And while I gaze, thy mild and placid light
  Sheds a soft calm upon my troubled breast;
And oft I think – fair planet of the night,
  That in thy orb, the wretched may have rest:
The sufferers of the earth perhaps may go,
  Released by death – to thy benignant sphere,
And the sad children of despair and woe
  Forget in thee, their cup of sorrow here.
Oh! that I soon may reach thy world serene,
Poor wearied pilgrim – in this toiling scene!

Charlotte Smith (1749–1806)

12ᵀᴴ JANUARY

The King of the Wood

Winter: winter in the woods
Is the bone that was the beauty,
The bough that lives the leaf:
The food supplies sink low
And the hedgehog and badger know the hour is late.

Comes snow – the scouting flakes
Nipping out of the north
Followed by bulky brigades
Falling with formidable lust
On land where evil and warm the weevil sleeps.

Spring: the leaves of the chestnut
Hang in the branches like bats;
Bluebells flood into valleys
Where butterflies dry wet wings
And the cock bird lords it in song on his terrain.

This is the season of primrose,
Woodruff, and anemone –
And the season of caterpillars
Of the mottled umber moth
Fattening ambition in a thousand worlds of plenty.

Summer: welcome the woods
When the air sweats in the sun!
Here is a draught of shade
In a cellar deep and dark
Where barrels are so tall they sway like trees.

Now ants are on the hunt
Each for a swag of syrup –
And the felted beech coccus
Seeks out the straight young tree
To lay the foundation stone of a leaning tower.

Autumn: the sky more blue
Than any flower or crystal:
The yellow and wrinkled face
Of the wood is streaked with wounds
As the catkins of the birches slide to the soil.

Burgled boxes with ermine
Lining drop their conkers
Among loot of acorns for squirrels –
And into the earth descends
The cockchafer beetle's larva to mine a future.

Clifford Dyment (1914–1971)

13TH JANUARY

To Winter

'O Winter! bar thine adamantine doors:
The north is thine; there hast thou built thy dark
Deep-founded habitation. Shake not thy roofs
Nor bend thy pillars with thine iron car.'

He hears me not, but o'er the yawning deep
Rides heavy; his storms are unchain'd, sheathèd
In ribbèd steel; I dare not lift mine eyes;
For he hath rear'd his sceptre o'er the world.

Lo! now the direful monster, whose skin clings
To his strong bones, strides o'er the groaning rocks:
He withers all in silence, and in his hand
Unclothes the earth, and freezes up frail life.

He takes his seat upon the cliffs, - the mariner
Cries in vain. Poor little wretch, that deal'st
With storms! – till heaven smiles, and the monster
Is driv'n yelling to his caves beneath mount Hecla.

William Blake (1757–1827)

14TH JANUARY

At Carbis Bay

FROM *INTERMEZZO: PASTORAL*

Out of the night of the sea,
Out of the turbulent night,
A sharp and hurrying wind
Scourges the waters white:
The terror by night.

Out of the doubtful dark,
Out of the night of the land,
What is it breathes and broods
Hoveringly at hand?
The menace of land.

Out of the night of heaven,
Out of the delicate sky,
Pale and serene the stars
In their silence reply:
The peace of the sky.

Arthur Symons (1865–1945)

15TH JANUARY

Snowdrop

Now is the globe shrunk tight
Round the mouse's dulled wintering heart.
Weasel and crow, as if moulded in brass,
Move through an outer darkness
Not in their right minds,
With the other deaths. She, too, pursues her ends,
Brutal as the stars of this month,
Her pale head heavy as metal.

Ted Hughes (1930–1998)

16TH JANUARY

There's a Certain Slant of Light

There's a certain Slant of light,
Winter Afternoons –
That oppresses, like the Heft
Of Cathedral Tunes –

Heavenly Hurt, it gives us –
We can find no scar,
But internal difference –
Where the Meanings, are –

None may teach it – Any –
'Tis the Seal Despair –
An imperial affliction
Sent us of the Air –

When it comes, the Landscape listens –
Shadows – hold their breath –
When it goes, 'tis like the Distance
On the look of Death –

Emily Dickinson (1830–1886)

17ᵀᴴ JANUARY

Evening by the Sea

It was between the night and day,
  The trees looked very weary – one by one
Against the west they seemed to sway,
  And yet were steady. The sad sun
In a sick doubt of colour lay
  Across the water's belt of dun.

On the weak wind scarce flakes of foam
  There floated, hardly bourne at all
From the rent edge of water – some
  Between slack gusts the wind let fall,
The white brine could not overcome
  That pale grass on the southern wall.

That evening one could always hear
  The sharp hiss of the shingle, rent
As each wave settled heavier,
  The same rough way. This noise was blent
With many sounds that hurt the air
  As the salt sea-wind came and went.

Algernon Charles Swinburne (1837–1909)

18TH JANUARY

Winter with the Gulf Stream

The boughs, the boughs are bare enough
But earth has never felt the snow.
Frost-furred our ivies are and rough

With bills of rime the brambles shew.
The hoarse leaves crawl on hissing ground
Because the sighing wind is low.

But if the rain-blasts be unbound
And from dank feathers wring the drops
The clogged brook runs with choking sound

Kneading the mounded mire that stops
His channel under clammy coats
Of foliage fallen in the copse.

A simple passage of weak notes
Is all the winter bird dare try.
The bugle moon by daylight floats

So glassy white about the sky,
So like a berg of hyaline,
And pencilled blue so daintily,

I never saw her so divine.
But through black branches, rarely drest
In scarves of silky shot and shine,

The webbed and the watery west
Where yonder crimson fireball sits
Looks laid for feasting and for rest.

I see long reefs of violets
In beryl-covered fens so dim,
A gold-water Pactolus frets

Its brindled wharves and yellow brim,
The waxen colours weep and run,
And slendering to his burning rim

Into the flat blue mist the sun
Drops out and all our day is done.

Gerard Manley Hopkins (1844–1889)

19TH JANUARY

The Two-Part Prelude

LINES 164–169

The leafless trees and every icy crag
Tinkled like iron; while the distant hills
Into the tumult sent an alien sound
Of melancholy, not unnoticed; while the stars,
Eastward, were sparkling clear, and in the west
The orange sky of evening died away.

William Wordsworth (1770–1850)

20TH JANUARY

Winter Morning

All is so still;
The hill a picture of a hill
With silver kine that glimmer
Now whiter and now dimmer
Through the fog's monochrome,
Painted by Cotman or Old Crome.

Pale in the sky
The winter sun shows a round eye,
That darkens and still brightens;
And all the landscape lightens
Till on the melting meadows
The trees are seen with hard white shadows.

Though in the balk
Ice doubles every lump of chalk
And the frost creeps across
The matted leaves in silver moss,
Here where the grass is dank
The sun weeps on this brightening bank.

Andrew Young (1885–1971)

21ST JANUARY

January Dusk

Austere and clad in sombre robes of grey,
  With hands upfolded and with silent wings,
In unimpassioned mystery the day
  Passes; a lonely thrush its requiem sings.

The dust of night is tangled in the boughs
  Of leafless lime and lilac, and the pine
Grows blacker, and the star upon the brows
  Of sleep is set in heaven for a sign.

Earth's little weary peoples fall on peace
  And dream of breaking buds and blossoming,
Of primrose airs, of days of large increase,
  And all the coloured retinue of spring.

John Drinkwater (1882–1937)

22ND JANUARY

St Vincent's Day

Remember on St Vincent's Day,
If that the sun his beams display,
Be sure to mark his transient beam,
Which through the casement sheds a gleam;
For 'tis a token bright and clear
Of prosperous weather all the year.

Anon

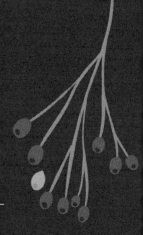

23ᴿᴰ JANUARY

A Frosty Day

Grass afield wears silver thatch;
   Palings all are edged with rime;
Frost-flowers pattern round the latch;
   Cloud nor breeze dissolve the clime;

When the waves are solid floor,
   And the clods are iron-bound,
And the boughs are crystall'd hoar,
   And the red leaf nailed a-ground.

When the fieldfare's flight is slow,
   And a rosy vapour rim,
Now the sun is small and low,
   Belts along the region dim.

When the ice-crack flies and flaws,
   Shore to shore, with thunder shock,
Deeper than the evening daws,
   Clearer than the village clock.

When the rusty blackbird strips,
  Bunch by bunch, the coral thorn;
And the pale day-crescent dips,
  Now to heaven, a slender horn.

Lord de Tabley (1835–1895)

24TH JANUARY

Winter Trees

See the bare arms of the trees!
Ah, it is good that it is winter,
and all the fuss and struggle of leaves is over,
and we may step into the anonymity of winter.

It is good that it is winter,
and the trees are stripped of all the nonsense
   of leaves,
as one who has shed the pretentions of clothes
is bare unto the soul.

David Austin (1926–2018)

25TH JANUARY

Sheep in Winter

The sheep get up and make their many tracks
And bear a load of snow upon their backs
And gnaw the frozen turnip to the ground
With sharp quick bite and then go noising round
The boy that pecks the turnips all the day
And knocks his hands to keep the cold away
And laps his legs in straw to keep them warm
And hides behind the hedges from the storm
The sheep as tame as dogs go where he goes
And try to shake their fleeces from the snows
Then leave their frozen meal and wander round
The stubble stack that stands beside the ground
And lye all night and face the drizzling storm
And shun the hovel where they might be warm

John Clare (1793–1864)

26TH JANUARY

January

FROM *THE EARTHLY PARADISE*

From this dull rainy undersky and low,
This murky ending of a leaden day,
That never knew the sun, this half-thawed snow,
These tossing black boughs faint against the grey
Of gathering night, thou turnest, dear, away
Silent, but with thy scarce-seen kindly smile
Sent through the dusk my longing to beguile.

There, the lights gleam, and all is dark without!
And in the sudden change our eyes meet dazed –
O look, love, look again! the veil of doubt
Just for one flash, past counting, then was raised!
O eyes of heaven, as clear thy sweet soul blazed
On mine a moment! O come back again
Strange rest and dear amid the long dull pain!

Nay, nay, gone by! though there she sitteth still,
With wide grey eyes so frank and fathomless –
Be patient, heart, thy days they yet shall fill
With utter rest – Yea, now thy pain they bless,
And feed thy last hope of the world's redress –
O unseen hurrying rack! O wailing wind!
What rest and where go ye this night to find?

William Morris (1834–1896)

27TH JANUARY

Wind at Midnight

Naked night; black elms, pallid and streaming sky!
Alone with the passion of the Wind,
In a hollow of stormy sound lost and alone am I,
On beaten earth a lost, unmated mind,
Marvelling at the stars, few, strange, and bright,
That all this dark assault of surging air,
Wrenching the rooted wood, hunting the cloud
   of night,
As if it would tear all and nothing spare,
Leaves supreme in the height.

Against what laws, what laws, what powers invisible,
Unsought yet always found,
Cries this dumb passion, strains this wrestle of
   wild will,
With tiger-leaps that seem to shake the ground?
Is it the baffled, homeless, rebel wind's crying
Or storm from a profounder passion wrung?
Ah, heart of man, is it you, the old powers defying,
By far desires and terrible beauty stung,
Broken on laws unseen, in a starry world dying
Ignorant, tameless, young?

Laurence Binyon (1869–1943)

28TH JANUARY

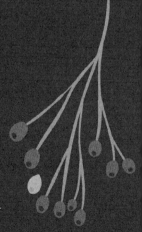

Seasons and Times

VERSES 1–5

Awhile in the dead of the winter,
The wind hurries keen through the sunshine,
But finds no more leaves that may linger
On tree-boughs to strew on the ground.

Long streaks of bright snow-drift, bank-shaded,
Yet lie on the slopes, under hedges;
But still all the road out to Thorndon
Would not wet a shoe on the ground.

The days, though the cold seems to strengthen,
Outlengthen their span, and the evening
Seeks later and later its westing,
To cast its dim hue on the ground,

Till tree-heads shall thicken their shadow
With leaves of a glittering greenness,
And daisies shall fold up their blossoms
At evening, in dew on the ground;

And then, in the plum-warding garden,
Or shadowy orchard, the house-man
Shall smile at his fruit, really blushing,
Where sunheat shoots through on the ground.

William Barnes (1801–1886)

29TH JANUARY

Snowdrop

A pale and pining girl, head bowed, heart gnawed,
whose figure nods and shivers in a shawl
of fine white wool, has suddenly appeared
in the damp woods, as mild and mute as snowfall.
She may not last. She has no strength at all,
but stoops and shakes as if she'd stood all night
on one bare foot, confiding with the moonlight.

One among several hundred clear-eyed ghosts
who get up in the cold and blink and turn
into those trembling emblems of night frosts,
she brings her burnt heart with her in an urn
of ashes, which she opens to re-mourn,
having no other outlet to express
her wild-flower sense of wounded gentleness.

Yes, she's no more now than a drop of snow
on a green stem – her name is now her calling.
Her mind is just a frozen melting glow
of water swollen to the point of falling
which maybe has no meaning. There's no telling.
But what's a beauty, what a mighty power
of patience kept intact is now in flower.

Alice Oswald (1966–)

30TH JANUARY

The Oak

VERSES 1 AND 2

What gnarlèd stretch, what depth of shade, is his!
  There needs no crown to mark the forest's king;
How in his leaves outshines full summer's bliss!
  Sun, storm, rain, dew, to him their tribute bring,
Which he with such benignant royalty
  Accepts, as overpayeth what is lent;
All nature seems his vassal proud to be,
  And cunning only for his ornament.

How towers he, too, amid the billowed snows,
  An unquelled exile from the summer's throne,
Whose plain, uncinctured front more kingly shows,
  Now that the obscuring courtier leaves are flown.
His boughs make music of the winter air,
  Jewelled with sleet, like some cathedral front
Where clinging snow-flakes with quaint art repair
  The dints and furrows of time's envious brunt.

James Russell Lowell (1819–1891)

31ˢᵀ JANUARY

The Song of the Beasts

(SUNG, ON ONE NIGHT, IN THE CITIES, IN THE DARKNESS)

Come away! Come away!
Ye are sober and dull through the common day,
But now it is night!
It is shameful night, and God is asleep!
(Have you not felt the quick fires that creep
Through the hungry flesh, and the lust of delight,
And hot secrets of dreams that day cannot say?) …
    The house is dumb;
The night calls out to you. – Come, ah, come!
Down the dim stairs, through the creaking door,
Naked, crawling on hands and feet
– It is meet! it is meet!
Ye are men no longer, but less and more,
Beast and God … Down the lampless street,
By little black ways, and secret places,
In the darkness and mire,
Faint laughter around, and evil faces
By the star-glint seen – ah! follow with us!
For the darkness whispers a blind desire,
And the fingers of night are amorous …

Keep close as we speed,
Though mad whispers woo you, and hot hands cling,
And the touch and the smell of bare flesh sting,
Soft flank by your flank, and side brushing side –
Tonight never heed!
Unswerving and silent follow with me,
Till the city ends sheer,
And the crook'd lanes open wide,
Out of the voices of night,
Beyond lust and fear,
To the level waters of moonlight,
To the level waters, quiet and clear,
To the black unresting plains of the calling sea.

Rupert Brooke (1887–1915)

FEBRUARY

Wild Skies and Flurrying Snows

1ST FEBRUARY

Midnight

There are sea and sky about me,
  And yet nothing sense can mark;
For a mist fills all the midnight
  Adding blindness to the dark.

There is not the faintest echo
  From the life of yesterday:
  Not the vaguest stir foretelling
Of a morrow on the way.

'Tis negation's hour of triumph
  In the absence of the sun;
'Tis the hour of endings, ended,
  Of beginnings, unbegun.

Yet the voice of awful silence
  Bids my waiting spirit hark;
There is action in the stillness,
  There is progress in the dark.

In the drift of things and forces
   Comes the better from the worse;
Swings the whole of Nature upward,
   Wakes, and thinks – a universe.

There will be more life tomorrow,
   And of life, more life that knows;
Though the sum of force be constant
   Yet the Living ever grows.

So we sing of evolution,
   And step strongly on our ways;
And we live through nights in patience
   And we learn the worth of days.

Louisa Bevington (1845–1895)

2ND FEBRUARY

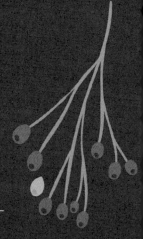

The Thrush in February

VERSES 1–5

I know him, February's thrush,
And loud at eve he valentines
On sprays that paw the naked bush
Where soon will sprout the thorns and bines.

Now ere the foreign singer thrills
Our vale his plain-song pipe he pours,
A herald of the million bills;
And heed him not, the loss is yours.

My study, flanked with ivied fir
And budded beech with dry leaves curled,
Perched over yew and juniper,
He neighbours, piping to his world: –

The wooded pathways dank on brown,
The branches on grey cloud a web,
The long green roller of the down,
An image of the deluge-ebb: –

And farther, they may hear along
The stream beneath the poplar row.
By fits, like welling rocks, the song
Spouts of a blushful Spring in flow.

George Meredith (1828–1909)

3RD FEBRUARY

Moon of Half-candied Meres

Moon of half-candied meres
And flurrying, fading snows;
Moon of unkindly rains,
Wild skies, and troubled vanes;
When the Norther snarls and bites,
And the lone moon walks a-cold,
And the lawns grizzle o' nights,
And wet fogs search the fold:
Here in this heart of mine
A dream that warms like wine,
A dream one other knows,
Moon of the roaring weirs
And the sip-sopping close,
   February Fill-Dyke,
Shapes like a royal rose –
   A red, red rose!

O, but the distance clears!
O, but the daylight grows!
Soon shall the pied wind-flowers
Babble of greening hours,
Primrose and daffodil
Yearn to a fathering sun,
The lark have all his will,
The thrush be never done,
And April, May, and June
Go to the same blythe tune
As this blythe dream of mine!
Moon when the crocus peers,
Moon when the violet blows,
    February Fair-Maid,
Haste, and let come the rose –
    Let come the rose!

W. E. Henley (1849–1903)

4ᵀᴴ FEBRUARY

The Tide Rises, the Tide Falls

The tide rises, the tide falls,
The twilight darkens, the curlew calls;
Along the sea-sands damp and brown
The traveller hastens toward the town,
　And the tide rises, the tide falls.

Darkness settles on roofs and walls,
But the sea, the sea in the darkness calls;
The little waves, with their soft, white hands,
Efface the footprints in the sands,
　And the tide rises, the tide falls.

The morning breaks; the steeds in their stalls
Stamp and neigh, as the hostler calls;
The day returns, but nevermore
Returns the traveller to the shore,
　And the tide rises, the tide falls.

Henry Wadsworth Longfellow (1807–1882)

5TH FEBRUARY

A Winter Piece

LINES 57–70

But winter has yet brighter scenes, – he boasts
Splendours beyond what gorgeous summer knows;
Or autumn with his many fruits, and woods
All flushed with many hues. Come, when the rains
Have glazed the snow, and clothed the trees
  with ice;
While the slant sun of February pours
Into the bowers a flood of light. Approach!
The encrusted surface shall upbear thy steps,
And the broad arching portals of the grove
Welcome thy entering. Look! the massy trunks
Are cased in the pure chrystal, each light spray,
Nodding and tinkling in the breath of heaven,
Is studded with its trembling water-drops,
That stream with rainbow radiance as they move.

William Cullen Bryant (1794–1878)

6TH FEBRUARY

Chamber Music XXXV

All day I hear the noise of waters
  Making moan,
Sad as the sea-bird is when, going
  Forth alone,
He hears the winds cry to the waters'
  Monotone.

The grey winds, the cold winds are blowing
  Where I go.
I hear the noise of many waters
  Far below.
All day, all night, I hear them flowing
  To and fro.

James Joyce (1882–1941)

7TH FEBRUARY

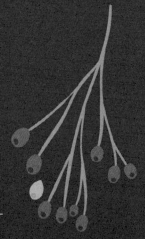

Sonnet: To Tartar, a Terrier Beauty

Snowdrop of dogs, with ear of brownest dye,
Like the last orphan leaf of naked tree
Which shudders in black autumn; though by thee,
Of hearing careless and untutored eye,
Not understood articulate speech of men
Nor marked the artificial mind of books,
– The mortal's voice eternized by the pen, –
Yet hast thou thought and language all unknown
To Babel's scholars; oft intensest looks,
Long scrutiny over some dark-veined stone
Dost thou bestow, learning dead mysteries
Of the world's birth-day, oft in eager tone
With quick-tailed fellows bandiest prompt replies,
Solicitudes canine, four-footed amities.

Thomas Lovell Beddoes (1803–1849)

8TH FEBRUARY

The Blue Bell is the Sweetest Flower

The blue bell is the sweetest flower
That waves in summer air:
Its blossoms have the mightiest power
To soothe my spirit's care.

There is a spell in purple heath
Too wildly, sadly dear;
The violet has a fragrant breath
But fragrance will not cheer.

The trees are bare, the sun is cold,
And seldom, seldom seen;
The heavens have lost their zone of gold
The earth its robe of green.

And ice upon the glancing stream
Has cast its sombre shade
And distant hills and valleys seem
In frozen mist arrayed.

The blue bell cannot charm me now,
The heath has lost its bloom,

The violets in the glen below
They yield no sweet perfume

But though I mourn the heather-bell
'Tis better far, away;
I know how fast my tears would swell
To see it smile today.

And that wood flower that hides so shy
Beneath the mossy stone
Its balmy scent and dewy eye:
'Tis not for them I moan.

It is the slight and stately stem,
The blossom's silvery blue,
The buds hid like a sapphire gem
In sheaths of emerald hue.

'Tis these that breathe upon my heart
A calm and softening spell
That if it makes the tear-drop start
Has power to soothe as well.

Emily Brontë (1818–1848)

9TH FEBRUARY

The Gloom that Winter Casts

The gloom that winter casts
  How soon the heart forgets –
When summer brings at last –
  The sun that never sets.
So love – when hope first gleams
  Forgets its former pain –
Amidst those sunny beams
  Which ne'er shall set again.

Edward Lear (1812–1888)

10TH FEBRUARY

What Makes Summer?

LINES 1–24

Winter froze both brook and well;
Fast and fast the snowflakes fell;
Children gathered round the hearth
Made a summer of their mirth;
When a boy, so lately come
That his life was yet one sum
Of delights – of aimless rambles,
Romps and dreams and games and gambols,
Thought aloud: 'I wish I knew
What makes summer – that I do!'
Father heard, and it did show him
How to write a little poem.

What makes summer, little one,
Do you ask? It is the sun.
Want of heat is all the harm,
Summer is but winter warm.
'Tis the sun – yes, that one there,
Dim and gray, low in the air!
Now he looks at us askance,
But will lift his countenance
Higher up, and look down straighter.
Rise much earlier, set much later,
Till we sing out, 'Hail, Well-comer,
Thou hast brought our own old Summer!'

George MacDonald (1824–1905)

11ᵀᴴ FEBRUARY

February Twilight

I stood beside a hill
    Smooth with new-laid snow,
A single star looked out
    From the cold evening glow.

There was no other creature
    That saw what I could see –
I stood and watched the evening star
    As long as it watched me.

Sara Teasdale (1884–1933)

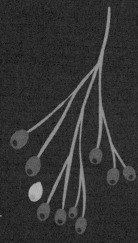

12TH FEBRUARY

A Robin

Ghost-grey the fall of night,
  Ice-bound the lane,
Lone in the dying light
  Flits he again;
Lurking where shadows steal,
Perched in his coat of blood,
Man's homestead at his heel,
  Death-still the wood.

Odd restless child; it's dark;
  All wings are flown
But this one wizard's – hark!
  Stone clapped on stone!
Changeling and solitary,
Secret and sharp and small,
Flits he from tree to tree,
  Calling on all.

Walter de la Mare (1873–1956)

13ᵀᴴ FEBRUARY

Sonnet

Bright star, would I were steadfast as thou art –
  Not in lone splendour hung aloft the night
And watching, with eternal lids apart,
  Like nature's patient, sleepless Eremite,
The moving waters at their priestlike task
  Of pure ablution round earth's human shores,
Or gazing on the new soft-fallen mask
  Of snow upon the mountains and the moors –
No – yet still steadfast, still unchangeable,
  Pillowed upon my fair love's ripening breast,
To feel for ever its soft fall and swell,
  Awake for ever in a sweet unrest,
Still, still to hear her tender-taken breath,
  And so live ever – or else swoon to death.

John Keats (1795–1821)

14TH FEBRUARY

The Secret

In the profoundest ocean
There is a rainbow shell,
It is always there, shining most stilly
Under the greatest storm waves
And under the happy little waves
That the old Greek called 'ripples of laughter'
And you listen, the rainbow shell
Sings – in the profoundest ocean.
It is always there, singing most silently!

Katherine Mansfield (1888–1923)

15TH FEBRUARY

The Mountain

The burn ran blacker for the snow
And ice-floe on ice-floe
Jangled in heavy lurches
Beneath the claret-coloured birches.

Dark grouse rose becking from the ground
And deer turned sharp heads round,
The antlers on their brows
Like stunted trees with withered boughs.

I climbed to where the mountain sloped
And long wan bubbles groped
Under the ice's cover,
A bridge that groaned as I crossed over.

I reached the mist, brighter than day,
That showed a specious way
By narrow crumbling shelves,
Where rocks grew larger than themselves.

But when I saw the mountain's spire
Looming through that damp fire,
I left it unwon
And climbed down to the setting sun.

Andrew Young (1885–1971)

16TH FEBRUARY

Hope

O thrush, is it true?
  Your song tells
Of a world born anew,
Of fields gold with buttercups, woodlands all blue
  With hyacinth bells;
Of primroses deep
  In the moss of the lane,
Of a Princess asleep
And dear magic to do.
Will the sun wake the princess? O thrush, is it true?
  Will Spring come again?

Will Spring come again?
   Now at last
With soft shine and rain
Will the violet be sweet where the dead leaves
                              have lain?

   Will Winter be past?
In the brown of the copse
   Will white wind-flowers star through
Where the last oak-leaf drops?
   Will the daisies come too,
And the may and the lilac? Will Spring
                              come again?

   O thrush, is it true?

E. Nesbit (1858–1924)

17ᵀᴴ FEBRUARY

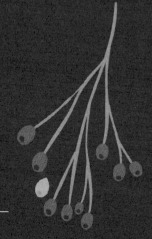

Water-Fowl

OBSERVED FREQUENTLY OVER THE LAKES
OF RYDAL AND GRASMERE

Mark how the feathered tenants of the flood,
With grace of motion that might scarcely seem
Inferior to angelical, prolong
Their curious pastime! shaping in mid air
(And sometimes with ambitious wing that soars
High as the level of the mountain-tops)
A circuit ampler than the lake beneath –
Their own domain; but ever, while intent
On tracing and retracing that large round,
Their jubilant activity evolves
Hundreds of curves and circlets, to and fro,
Upward and downward, progress intricate
Yet unperplexed, as if one spirit swayed
Their indefatigable flight. 'Tis done –
Ten times, or more, I fancied it had ceased;
But lo! the vanished company again
Ascending; they approach – I hear their wings,
Faint, faint at first; and then an eager sound,
Past in a moment – and as faint again!

They tempt the sun to sport amid their plumes;
They tempt the water, or the gleaming ice,
To show them a fair image; 'tis themselves,
Their own fair forms, upon the glimmering plain,
Painted more soft and fair as they descend
Almost to touch; – then up again aloft,
Up with a sally and a flash of speed,
As if they scorned both resting-place and rest!

William Wordsworth (1770–1850)

18TH FEBRUARY

In Dark Weather

Against the gaunt, brown-purple hill
The bright brown oak is brown and bare;
A pale-brown flock is feeding there –
    Contented, still.

No bracken lights the bleak hill-side;
No leaves are on the branches wide;
No lambs across the fields have cried;
    – Not yet.

But whorl by whorl the green fronds climb;
The ewes are patient till their time;
The warm buds swell beneath the rime –
    For life does not forget.

Mary Webb (1881–1927)

19TH FEBRUARY

West Wind in Winter

Another day awakes. And who –
  Changing the world – is this?
He comes at whiles, the winter through,
  West Wind! I would not miss
His sudden tryst: the long, the new
  Surprises of his kiss.

Vigilant, I make haste to close
  With him who comes my way.
I go to meet him as he goes;
  I know his note, his lay,
His colour and his morning-rose,
  And I confess his day.

My window waits; at dawn I hark
  His call; at morn I meet
His haste around the tossing park
  And down the softened street;
The gentler light is his; the dark.
  The grey – he turns it sweet.

So too, so too, do I confess
   My poet when he sings.
He rushes on my mortal guess
   With his immortal things.
I feel, I know him. On I press –
   He finds me 'twixt his wings.

Alice Meynell (1847–1922)

20TH FEBRUARY

February

FROM *THE EARTHLY PARADISE*

The change has come at last, and from the west
Drives on the wind, and gives the clouds no rest,
And ruffles up the water thin that lies
Over the surface of the thawing ice;
Sunrise and sunset with no glorious show
Are seen, as late they were across the snow;
The wet-lipped west wind chilleth to the bone
More than the light and flickering east hath done.
Full soberly the earth's fresh hope begins,
Nor stays to think of what each new day wins:
And still it seems to bid us turn away
From this chill thaw to dream of blossomed May:

William Morris (1834–1896)

21ˢᵀ FEBRUARY

To Jane: The Invitation

LINES 1–46

Best and brightest, come away!
Fairer far than this fair Day,
Which, like thee to those in sorrow,
Comes to bid a sweet good-morrow
To the rough Year just awake
In its cradle on the brake
The brightest hour of unborn Spring,
Through the winter wandering,
Found, it seems, the halcyon Morn
To hoar February born.
Bending from Heaven, in azure mirth,
It kiss'd the forehead of the Earth,
And smiled upon the silent sea,
And bade the frozen streams be free,
And waked to music all their fountains,
And breathed upon the frozen mountains,
And like a prophetess of May
Strewed flowers upon the barren way,
Making the wintry world appear
Like one on whom thou smilest, dear
Away, away, from men and towns,
To the wild wood and the downs –
To the silent wilderness

Where the soul need not repress
Its music lest it should not find
An echo in another's mind,
While the touch of Nature's art
Harmonizes heart to heart.
I leave this notice on my door
For each accustomed visitor: –
'I am gone into the fields
To take what this sweet hour yields; –
Reflection, you may come to-morrow,
Sit by the fireside with Sorrow. –
You with the unpaid bill, Despair, –
You, tiresome verse-reciter, Care, –
I will pay you in the grave, –
Death will listen to your stave.
Expectation too, be off!
To-day is for itself enough;
Hope, in pity mock not Woe
With smiles, nor follow where I go;
Long having lived on thy sweet food,
At length I find one moment's good
After long pain – with all your love,
That you never told me of.'

Percy Bysshe Shelley (1792–1822)

22ND FEBRUARY

Call for the Robin Redbreast and the Wren

Call for the robin-redbreast and the wren,
Since o'er shady groves they hover,
And with leaves and flowers do cover
The friendless bodies of unburied men.
Call unto his funeral dole
The ant, the field-mouse, and the mole,
To rear him hillocks that shall keep him warm
And, when gay tombs are robbed, sustain no harm;
But keep the wolf far thence, that's foe to men,
For with his nails he'll dig them up again.

John Webster (c.1580–c.1625)

23RD FEBRUARY

The Robin

The Robin is a Gabriel
In humble circumstances –
His Dress denotes him socially,
Of Transport's Working Classes –
He has the punctuality
Of the New England Farmer –
The same oblique integrity,
A Vista vastly warmer –

A small but sturdy Residence
A self denying Household,
The Guests of Perspicacity
Are all that cross his Threshold –
As covert as a Fugitive,
Cajoling Consternation
By Ditties to the Enemy
And Sylvan Punctuation –

Emily Dickinson (1830–1886)

24TH FEBRUARY

Winter Heavens

Sharp is the night, but stars with frost alive
Leap off the rim of earth across the dome.
It is a night to make the heavens our home
More than the nest whereto apace we strive.
Lengths down our road each fir-tree seems a hive,
In swarms outrushing from the golden comb.
They waken waves of thoughts that burst to foam:
The living throb in me, the dead revive.
Yon mantle clothes us: there, past mortal breath,
Life glistens on the river of the death.
It folds us, flesh and dust; and have we knelt,
Or never knelt, or eyed as kine the springs
Of radiance, the radiance enrings:
And this is the soul's haven to have felt.

George Meredith (1828–1909)

25TH FEBRUARY

Craving for Spring

LINES 1–12

I wish it were spring in the world.

Let it be spring!
Come, bubbling, surging tide of sap!
Come, rush of creation!
Come, life! surge through this mass of
    mortification!
Come, sweep away these exquisite, ghastly
    first-flowers,
which are rather last-flowers!
Come, thaw down their cool portentousness,
    dissolve them:
snowdrops, straight, death-veined exhalations of
    white and purple crocuses,
flowers of the penumbra, issue of corruption,
    nourished in mortification,
jets of exquisite finality;
Come, spring, make havoc of them!

D. H. Lawrence (1885–1930)

26ᵀᴴ FEBRUARY

Thaw

Over the land freckled with snow half-thawed
The speculating rooks at their nests cawed
And saw from elm-tops, delicate as flower of grass,
What we below could not see, Winter pass.

Edward Thomas (1878–1917)

27TH FEBRUARY

Look Through the Naked Bramble and Black Thorn

Look through the naked bramble and black thorn
And see the arum show its vivid green
Glossy and rich and some ink spotted like the morn
Ing sky with clouds – in sweetest neuks I've been
And seen the arum sprout its happy green
Full of spring visions and green thoughts o' may
Dead leaves a' litter where its leaves are seen
Broader and brighter green from day to day
Beneath the hedges in their leafless spray

John Clare (1793–1864)

28TH FEBRUARY

The Door of Spring

How shall we open the door of Spring
  That Winter is holding wearily shut?
    Though winds are calling and waters brawling,
    And snow decaying and light delaying,
  Yet will it not move in its yielding rut
And back on its flowery hinges swing,
      Till wings are flapping
      And woodpeckers tapping
      With sharp, clear rapping
        At the door of Spring.

How shall we fasten the door of Spring
  Wide, so wide that it cannot close?
    Though buds are filling and frogs are trilling,
    And violets breaking and grass awaking,
  Yet doubtfully back and forth it blows
Till come the birds, and the woodlands ring
      With sharp beak stammer –
      The sudden clamor
      Of the woodpecker's hammer
        At the door of Spring.

Ethelwyn Wetherald (1857–1940)

29TH FEBRUARY

Winter's Turning

Snow is still on the ground,
But there is a golden brightness in the air.
Across the river,
Blue,
Blue,
Sweeping widely under the arches
Of many bridges,
Is a spire and a dome,
Clear as though ringed with ice-flakes,
Golden, and pink, and jocund.
On a near-by steeple,
A golden weather-cock flashes smartly,
His open beak 'Cock-a-doodle-dooing'
Straight at the ear of Heaven.
A tall apartment house,
Crocus-coloured,
Thrusts up from the street
Like a new-sprung flower.
Another street is edged and patterned
With the bloom of bricks,
Houses and houses of rose-red bricks,
Every window a-glitter.

The city is a parterre,
Blowing and glowing,
Alight with the wind,
Washed over with gold and mercury.
Let us throw up our hats,
For we are past the age of balls
And have none handy.
Let us take hold of hands,
And race along the sidewalks,
And dodge the traffic in crowded streets.
Let us whir with the golden spoke-wheels
Of the sun.
For to-morrow Winter drops into the
    waste-basket,
And the calendar calls it March.

Amy Lowell (1874–1925)

Index of first lines

Index of poets

Acknowledgements

As always, a huge thanks to everyone at Hatchards for looking after my books so well. Thanks to all my friends who made recommendations and Kristy Richardson, Nicola Newman and Tina Persaud at Batsford who are wonderful editors.

This was the time of year that Matilda, my small grey tabby cat, went missing for three months. The harshness that winter can bring has had particular meaning for me ever since. Without Mat and Sarah it would have been a much harder time. Happily she was rescued and resumed her duties as my paperweight.

p159: David Austin, 'Winter Trees' from *The Breathing Earth*, Enitharmon Press, 2014. Reprinted with permission of David Austin Roses.

p129–130: Clifford Dyment, 'The King of the Wood' from *Experiences and Places*, J M Dent, 1955.

p121: John Foster, 'The Lake' from *The Poetry Chest*, Oxford University Press, 2007. Reproduced with permission of the Licensor through PLSclear.

p69: Robert Frost, 'Stopping by Woods on a Snowy Evening', from *The Complete Poems*, Cape, 1951. Reprinted with permission of Penguin Random House.

p37: Elizabeth Jennings, 'Beech', from *Collected Poems of Elizabeth Jennings 1953-1985*, Carcanet, 1986. Reprinted by kind permission of David Higham Associates Ltd.